E
ROT

Rotner, Shelley

Senses at the seashore

Shelley Rotner

Senses at the Seashore

M Millbrook Press   Minneapolis

To my parents and our shared love of the ocean—S. R.

Millbrook Press
A division of Lerner Publishing Group
241 First Avenue North
Minneapolis, Minnesota 55401 U.S.A.

Website address: www.lernerbooks.com

Rotner, Shelley.
Senses at the seashore / Shelley Rotner.
p. cm.
Summary: A child shares the sights, sounds, smells, touches, and tastes of a day at the seashore.
ISBN-13: 978-0-7613-2897-1 (lib. bdg. : alk. paper)
ISBN-10: 0-7613-2897-1 (lib. bdg. : alk. paper)
[1. Seashore—Fiction. 2. Senses and sensation—Fiction.] I. Title.
PZ7.R752Se 2006
[E]—dc22   2005006151

Manufactured in the United States of America
1 2 3 4 5 6 - DP - 11 10 09 08 07 06

At the seashore . . .

See the blue water.

Hear
the waves
crash.

Smell
the
lotion.

Touch the cold water.

Taste the salty seawater.

See

a fishing boat
go by.

Smell
the fresh fish.

Touch the warm sand.

Hear
the seashell.

Taste
your yummy
sandwich.

Smell the roses in bloom.

Hear the gulls cry.

Touch
a soft feather.

See the fluffy white clouds.

Taste a fruity pop.

See a kite flying high.

Smell the seaweed at low tide.

Touch its slippery surface.

Hear
the lifeguard's whistle.

Taste
the sweet juicy
watermelon.

Hear
your
parents
call.

Smell
the bonfire.

Touch the fluffy towel.

Taste your delicious dinner.

See the sunset.

At the seashore, there's so much to
see, hear, smell, taste, touch.